Dad's Wit

summersdale

DAD'S WIT

Copyright © Summersdale Publishers Ltd 2010

All rights reserved.

Illustrations by Ian Baker

Summersdale Publishers Ltd
46 West Street
Chichester
West Sussex
PO19 1RP
UK

www.summersdale.com

Printed and bound in Great Britain

ISBN: 978-1-84953-078-1

Disclaimer
Every effort has been made to attribute the quotations in this collection to the correct source. Should there be any omissions or errors in this respect we apologise and shall be pleased to make the appropriate acknowledgements in any future edition.

Substantial discounts on bulk quantities of Summersdale books are available to corporations, professional associations and other organisations. For details contact Summersdale Publishers by telephone: +44 (0) 1243 771107, fax: +44 (0) 1243 786300 or email: nicky@summersdale.com.

Dad's

Wit

Quips and Quotes for
Fantastic Fathers

Richard Benson

Illustrations by Ian Baker

Contents

Editor's Note

Head of the household or family cabbie? Breadwinner or barbecue-only chef? Soft touch or tyrant? A father has many guises and being a dad provides a lifetime of magic moments, from showing your little 'un how to score a goal in the back garden and being looked up to as a hero (commonly stops at about eleven years old!), to dancing the funky chicken at your child's leaving home bash and being the strong shoulder to cry on when things go wrong.

This collection is a celebration of why it's great to be a father. Even when they all seem to think you're just a bit silly, dad always has wise words to impart. No one is too old to need their dad.

And for all those new dads out there, apparently the secret of successful fatherhood is 'to know when to stop tickling'!

FROM HERE TO PATERNITY

Oh, what a tangled web we weave when first we practise to conceive.

Don Herold

Children are nature's very
own form of birth control.

Dave Barry

The problem with the gene pool
is that there is no lifeguard.

Steven Wright

Every ten seconds, there is a
woman giving birth to a child. She
must be found and stopped.

Sam Levenson

I feel cheated never being able to
know what it's like to get pregnant,
carry a child and breastfeed.

Dustin Hoffman

A ship under sail and a
big-bellied woman,
Are the handsomest two things
that can be seen common.

Benjamin Franklin

It is much easier to become
a father than to be one.

Kent Nerburn

I like children. If they're
properly cooked.

W. C. Fields

We have no children, except me.

Brendan Behan when asked if he had children

Why are men reluctant to become fathers? They aren't through being children.

Cindy Garner

❦

Is it to prove they had sex once?

Jeremy Hardy questioning why a man would want to be a father

I've got more paternity suits than leisure suits.

Engelbert Humperdinck

Parenthood is a lot easier
to get into than out of.

Bruce Lansky

Families with babies and
families without babies are
sorry for each other.

Ed Howe

L-PLATES

To be a successful father... there's one absolute rule: when you have a kid, don't look at it for the first two years.

Ernest Hemingway

Babies are always more trouble than you thought – and more wonderful.

Charles Osgood

❧

When you become a father, you get scared about everything.

Alex Trebek

❧

The worst feature of a new baby is its mother's singing.

Kin Hubbard

Some people have got advice, some people have got horror stories. I like people that look you in the eye with a glow and say, 'It's gonna be cool.'

Russell Crowe on impending fatherhood

A baby is an inestimable blessing and bother.

Mark Twain

The most extraordinary thing about having a child is people think I'm a responsible human being.

Colin Farrell

It's like washing dishes, but imagine if the dishes were your kids, so you really love the dishes.

Chris Martin on why changing nappies is so rewarding

When you are dealing with a
child, keep all your wits about
you, and sit on the floor.

Austin O'Malley

The toughest job in the world isn't
being a president. It's being a parent.

Bill Clinton

THE GREATEST DAY
OF YOUR LIFE

My daughter was
born under a lucky
star. Lionel Blair lived
in the flat above us.

Bob Monkhouse

The way events are shaping,
they'll be lucky to be present
at the conception.

**George H. Davies on the fuss about fathers
being present at the birth of their children**

Although present on the occasion,
I have no clear recollection of
the events leading up to it.

Winston Churchill on his own birth

On the one hand we will never experience childbirth. On the other hand, we can open all our own jars.

Bruce Willis on the pros and cons of being a man

If men had to have babies, they would only ever have one each.

Princess Diana

A home birth is
preferable. That way
you're not missing
anything on television.

Jeremy Hardy

You can tell it's a journalist's child because all he wants to do is to drink and sleep.

John Humphrys on the birth of his third child

———◆———

This moment of meeting seemed to be a birth time for both of us: her first and my second life.

Laurie Lee

———◆———

All babies are supposed to look like me – at both ends.

Winston Churchill

I was so ugly that the midwife
took one look at me, turned,
and slapped my father.

Rodney Dangerfield

They can if you hit them
in the goolies with a cricket
bat for fourteen hours.

**Jo Brand on the notion that men can't
experience the pain of childbirth**

I remember so clearly us going into hospital so Victoria could have Brooklyn. I was eating a Lion bar at the time.

David Beckham

———◆———

Speech-making is exactly like childbirth. You are so glad to get it over with.

John Barrymore

———◆———

... a little like watching a wet St Bernard coming in through the cat door.

Jeff Foxworthy on the birth of a child

IT DOESN'T COME
WITH A MANUAL

Try to get one that
doesn't spit up.
Other than that,
you're on your own.

Calvin Trillin, *Family Man*

A truly appreciative child will break, lose, spoil, or fondle to death any really successful gift within a matter of minutes.

Russell Lynes

❖

Children really brighten up a household. They never turn the lights off.

Ralph Bus

❖

Fathering is not something perfect men do, but something that perfects the man.

Frank Pittman, *Man Enough*

The hand that rocks the cradle
usually is attached to someone
who isn't getting enough sleep.

John Fiebig

———•———

Children are like wet cement.
Whatever falls on them
makes an impression.

Dr Haim Ginott

The trouble with
learning to parent on
the job is that your
child is the teacher.

Robert Brault

When I was a boy of fourteen, my
father was so ignorant I could hardly
stand to have the old man around.
But when I got to be twenty-one,
I was astonished at how much he
had learned in seven years.

Mark Twain

Did you know babies are nauseated
by the smell of a clean shirt?

Jeff Foxworthy

There are 152 distinctly different ways – and all are right.

Heywood Brown on how to hold a baby

Everybody knows how to raise children, except the people who have them.

P. J. O'Rourke

A two-year-old is kind of like having a blender, but you don't have a top for it.

Jerry Seinfeld

I learned the way a monkey learns
– by watching its parents.

Prince Charles

Child-rearing myth number one:
labour ends when the baby is born.

Anonymous

Parenthood remains the greatest
single preserve of the amateur.

Alvin Toffler

You can learn many things from children. How much patience you have, for instance.

Franklin P. Jones

I was the same kind of father as I was a harpist – I played by ear.

Harpo Marx

DADDY'S LITTLE PRINCESS

My finger may
be small, but I
can still wrap my
daddy around it.

Anonymous

She got her looks from her
father. He's a plastic surgeon.

Groucho Marx

If I wanted something from my father,
I would put my little feet together
pigeon-toe style, tilt my head and
smile. I got what I wanted every time.

Shirley MacLaine

41

The first man a girl falls in
love with is her daddy.

Anonymous

A son is a son till he takes
him a wife, a daughter is a
daughter all of her life.

Irish saying

Are we not like two
volumes of one book?

Marceline Desbordes-Valmore

I've learned more from my daughter
than she has learned from me.

Antonio Banderas

My father was often angry
when I was most like him.

Lillian Hellman

'Margo, don't be a sheep. People hate sheep. They eat sheep.'

Margo Kaufman on her dad's advice after she
complained to him that she didn't fit in

Nobody in this world can make me so happy or so miserable as you.

Thomas Jefferson in a letter to his
eldest daughter Martha

Little girls are the nicest things
that happen to people.

Allan Beck

It isn't that I'm a weak father, it's
just that she's a strong daughter!

Henry Fonda

... when his daughter puts her arm over his shoulder and says, 'Daddy, I need to ask you something,' he is a pat of butter in a hot frying pan.

Garrison Keillor

FATHERLY ADVICE

Never put anything
on paper, my boy,
and never trust a
man with a small
black moustache.

P. G. Wodehouse

My dad always used to tell me that
if they challenge you to an after-
school fight, tell them you won't wait
– you can kick their ass right now.

Cameron Diaz

My father always told me, 'Find
a job you love and you'll never
have to work a day in your life.'

Jim Fox

My father always used to say that
when you die, if you've got five real
friends, then you've had a great life.

Lee Iacocca

I have found the best way to
give advice to your children is
to find out what they want and
then advise them to do it.

Harry S. Truman

Never get a tattoo because if you turn to a life of crime you're easily identifiable.

Amy Lamé on the number one piece of advice that her father gave her

My father told me that if I saw a
man in a Rolls Royce one could
be sure he wasn't a gentleman
unless he was a chauffeur.

Earl of Arran

Dad taught me everything I
know. Unfortunately, he didn't
teach me everything he knows.

Al Unser Jr

Always be a little kinder
than necessary.

J. M. Barrie

Ask your mother.

Frank Lancaster's advice to his children

Father told me that if I ever met
a lady in a dress like yours, I must
look her straight in the eyes.

Prince Charles

My father was fond of saying,
'Better to keep your mouth closed
and be thought a fool than to
open it and remove all doubt.'

Carol Thatcher

Don't criticise what you don't
understand, son. You never
walked in that man's shoes.

Elvis Presley

Son, never throw a
punch at a redwood.

Tom Selleck

My father would say, 'Do the best
you can. And then the hell with it.'

Ted Kennedy

My father used to say, 'Let them see you and not the suit. That should be secondary.'

Cary Grant

HERO WORSHIP

Dad... a son's
first hero.

Anonymous

You don't raise heroes; you raise
sons. And if you treat them like
sons, they'll turn out to be heroes,
even if it's just in your own eyes.

Walter Schirra Sr

For many people, God is
just dad with a mask on.

Anonymous

My daddy, he was somewhere
between God and John Wayne.

Hank Williams Jr

His heritage to his children wasn't words or possessions, but an unspoken treasure, the treasure of his example as a man and a father.

Will Rogers Jr

I've had a hard life, but my hardships are nothing against the hardships that my father went through in order to get me to where I started.

Bartrand Hubbard

Dads are stone
skimmers,
mud wallowers,
water wallopers,
ceiling swoopers,
shoulder gallopers,
upsy-downsy, over-
and-through, round-
and-about whoosers.

Helen Thomson

Nothing could get at me if I
curled up on my father's lap...
All about him was safe.

Naomi Mitchison

The father who would taste the
essence of his fatherhood must...
begin again beside his child, marching
step by step over the same old road.

Angelo Patri

... my dad is my hero. I'm never free of a problem nor do I truly experience a joy until we share it.

Nancy Sinatra

———◆———

Directly after God in heaven comes a Papa.

Wolfgang Amadeus Mozart

———◆———

I set the bar at half of my dad. If I could get that far, I'd consider my life successful.

Jeb Bush

CAN'T LIVE WITH THEM;
CAN'T LIVE
WITHOUT THEM

The one thing
children wear out
faster than shoes
is parents.

John J. Plomp

What is a home without
children? Quiet.

Henny Youngman

The only way for this father to
be certain of bathroom privacy
is to shave at the gas station.

Bill Cosby

They are the greatest joy in the
world. But they are also terrorists.

Ray Romano on having children

———•‹·›•———

Having one child makes you a
parent; having two you are a referee.

David Frost

———•‹·›•———

Having children makes you no
more a parent than having a
piano makes you a pianist.

Michael Levine

The trouble with being a parent
is that by the time you are
experienced, you are unemployed.

Anonymous

Humans are the only animals
that have children on purpose
with the exception of guppies,
who like to eat theirs.

P. J. O'Rourke

Insanity is hereditary – you
get it from your children.

Sam Levenson

The truth is that parents are
not really interested in justice.
They just want quiet.

Bill Cosby

The trouble with
children is that they
are not returnable.

Quentin Crisp

DEEP POCKETS

Money isn't
everything – but it sure
keeps you in touch
with your children.

Jean Paul Getty

A boy becomes a man when he stops asking his father for money and requests a loan.

Anonymous

It now costs more to amuse a child than it once did to educate his father.

Vaughan Monroe

For the first year,
you are only a
curiosity... after that,
an amusement park
ride. Then, a referee.
And, finally, a bank.

Esquire magazine, 'Things a Man
Should Know About Fatherhood'

My daughter wanted a new pair of trainers. I told her, 'You're eleven. Make your own!'

Jeremy Hardy

A father is a fellow who has replaced the currency in his wallet with snapshots of his kids.

Anonymous

A child, like your stomach, doesn't
need all you can afford to give it.

Frank A. Clark

A truly rich man is one whose
children run into his arms
when his hands are empty.

Anonymous

A father is a banker
provided by nature.

French proverb

If you want to recapture your
youth, just cut off his allowance.

Al Bernstein

That is the thankless position of the
father in the family – the provider
for all, and the enemy of all.

August Strindberg

Life was a lot simpler when what we
honoured was father and mother
rather than all major credit cards.

Robert Orben

Well, it's hard to
know what to get the
man who provides
everything.

Michael Feldman on receiving a set of
hose nozzles on Father's Day

SETTING A
GOOD EXAMPLE

Life doesn't come
with an instruction
book; that's why
we have fathers.

H. Jackson Brown Jr

Setting a good example for children
takes all the fun out of middle age.

William Feather

My best training came
from my father.

Thomas Woodrow Wilson

My father taught me to work;
he did not teach me to love it.

Abraham Lincoln

———◆———

Of course my father was a
great influence on me. He
taught me how to read.

Michael Foot

———◆———

The father who does not teach
his son his duties is equally guilty
as the son who neglects them.

Confucius

Our father used to
sit us on the po and
tell us ghost stories.

**Big O talking about his father's
alternatives to laxatives**

All children alarm their parents,
if only because you are forever
expecting to encounter yourself.

Gore Vidal

Children have never been very good
at listening to their elders, but they
have never failed to imitate them.

James Baldwin

The thing that impresses me
most about Americans is the way
parents obey their children.

Edward, Duke of Windsor

Few things are harder to put
up with than the annoyance
of a good example.

Mark Twain

If you must hold yourself up
to your children as an object
lesson, hold yourself up as a
warning and not as an example.

George Bernard Shaw

Setting too good an example is a
kind of slander seldom forgiven.

Benjamin Franklin

WHAT IS FATHERHOOD?

I make it a rule to
pat all children on
the head as they
pass by – in case
it is one of mine.

Augustus John

The secret of
fatherhood is to know
when to stop tickling.

Anonymous

A father is a giant from whose
shoulders you can see for ever.

Perry Garfinkel

Up until I became a father, it was
all about self-obsession. But then
I learned exactly what it's all about:
the delight of being a servant.

Eric Clapton

Being a father is like doing drugs
– you smell bad, get no sleep and
spend all your money on them.

Paul Bettany

There are three stages of a man's
life: he believes in Santa Claus,
he doesn't believe in Santa
Claus, he is Santa Claus.

Anonymous

A father is a man who
expects his children to be as
good as he meant to be.

Carol Coats

—

Being a dad is the new black.

Laurence Llewellyn-Bowen

—

Fathering is the most masculine
thing a man can do.

Frank Pittman

Fathers embody a delicious
mixture of familiarity and novelty;
they are novel without being
strange or frightening.

Louise J. Kaplan

Infinite patience, boundless
enthusiasm, kindness, the ability to
score a goal... and the strength to
say 'NO' every now and again.

Piers Morgan on what it takes to be a good father

Fathers, like mothers, are not born. Men grow into fathers – and fathering is a very important stage in their development.

David M. Gottesman

Dads regard themselves a giant shock absorber, there to protect the family from the ruts and bumps on the road of life.

W. Bruce Cameron, *8 Simple Rules for Dating My Teenage Daughter*

[A father is] chock-full of qualms and romantic terrors, believing change is a threat... like your first shoes with heels on.

Phyllis McGinley

SHE'S GROWING
UP FAST!

Watching your
daughter being
collected by her date
feels like handing
over a million-dollar
Stradivarius to a gorilla.

Jim Bishop

A father is always making his baby
into a little woman. And when she is
a woman he turns her back again.

Enid Bagnold

The night I announced I was
getting married, Daddy paced
for hours on the porch.

Loretta Lynn

I will look them up and down... I'll have the sword out and demand, 'What do you want from her?'

Antonio Banderas

Many a man wishes he were strong enough to tear a telephone book in half – especially if he has a teenage daughter.

Guy Lombardo

Daughters are like flowers,
they fill the world with beauty,
and sometimes attract pests.

Anonymous

———•———

A doting father is not simply
surprised when his little girl
grows up, he is crushed.

Anonymous

———•———

I figure if I kill the first one,
word will get out.

Charles Barkley on his 12-year-old
daughter's future boyfriends

I have three
daughters and I find
as a result I played
King Lear almost
without rehearsal.

Peter Ustinov

DAD VS MUM

My mother taught me my ABCs. From my father I learned the glories of going to the bathroom outside.

Lewis Grizzard

You don't have to deserve your mother's love. You have to deserve your father's. He's more particular.

Robert Frost

———

You know the problem with men? After the birth, we're irrelevant.

Dustin Hoffman

———

Small boy's definition of Father's Day: It's just like Mother's Day only you don't spend so much.

Anonymous

The most important thing a
father can do for his children
is to love their mother.

Henry Ward Beecher

Children always know when
company is in the living room
– they can hear their mother
laughing at their father's jokes.

Anonymous

Mommy would never divorce Daddy.
He's just like one of the family.

Bill Keane

Somebody said that no one can
love a child the way a mother can.
Somebody was never a father.

Anonymous

Mothers are a biological necessity;
fathers are a social invention.

Margaret Mead

A good father is a little
bit of a mother.

Lee Salk

My kids hate me. Every Father's
Day they give a 'World's Greatest
Dad' mug to the milkman.

Rodney Dangerfield

I'm a fun father, but not a good
father. The hard decisions
always went to my wife.

John Lithgow

GROWING PAINS

A lot of parents pack
up their troubles
and send them off
to summer camp.

Raymond Duncan

When I was a kid, I said to my father one afternoon, 'Daddy, will you take me to the zoo?' He answered, 'If the zoo wants you, let them come and get you.'

Jerry Lewis

The worst waste of breath, next to playing a saxophone, is advising a son.

Kin Hubbard

End the name of your child
with a vowel... when you
yell, the name will carry.

Bill Cosby

A child enters your home... makes so
much noise you can hardly stand it.
The child departs, leaving the house
so silent you think you are going mad.

John Andrew Holmes

The children despise their parents
until the age of forty, when they
suddenly become just like them
– thus preserving the system.

Quentin Crewe

Parents were invented to
make children happy by giving
them something to ignore.

Ogden Nash

Explain the concept
of death very carefully
to your child. This
will make threatening
him with it much
more effective.

P. J. O'Rourke

Raising children is like
chewing on a stone.

Arab proverb

Human beings are the only
creatures on earth that allow their
children to come back home.

Bill Cosby

Never underestimate a child's
ability to get into more trouble.

Martin Mull

Your children tell you casually years
later what it would have killed you
with worry to know at the time.

Mignon McLaughlin

It's occasionally maddening to
see your children doing the things
that you did that were stupid.

George Martin

THE BEST JOB IN
THE WORLD

I've made a few nice
dishes in my time,
but this has got to
be the best one
I've ever made.

Jamie Oliver talking about his first child

There's a time for being a rock star, on TV, and in the studio, but you've got to put time aside for being daddy, and getting chocolate rubbed in your face.

Noel Gallagher

Being a dad is more important than football.

David Beckham

What's a good
investment? Go home
from work early and
spend the afternoon
throwing a ball around
with your son.

Ben Stein

Happiness is having a large,
loving, caring, close-knit
family in another city.

George Burns

———

I figure somewhere between kid
number one and number seven,
I must have learned a few things.

Mel Gibson

Anyone who hasn't had children
doesn't know what life is.

Henry Miller, *My Life and Times*

A three-year-old child... gets
almost as much fun out of a
set of swings as it does out of
finding a small green worm.

Bill Vaughan

FAMILY MAN

Character is largely
caught, and the father
and the home should
be the great sources
of character infection.

Frank H. Cheley

I've got seven kids. The three words you hear most around my house are 'hello', 'goodbye' and 'I'm pregnant'.

Dean Martin

Families are like fudge – mostly sweet with a few nuts.

Anonymous

Having a family is like having a bowling alley installed in your head.

Martin Mull

You don't choose your
family. They are God's gift
to you, as you are to them.

Desmond Tutu

❧

Raising children is like making
biscuits: it is as easy to raise a
big batch as one, while you have
your hands in the dough.

E. W. Howe

❧

A man that doesn't spend time with
his family, can never be a real man.

Mario Puzo, *The Godfather*

When you have kids, it takes the
focus off you. You forget about
what clothes you're wearing,
or if you went to the gym.

James Denton

When our relatives are at
home, we have to think of all
their good points or it would be
impossible to endure them.

George Bernard Shaw

Children are a great comfort
in your old age – and they help
you reach it faster, too.

Lionel Kauffman

❦

There is no cure for laziness
but a large family helps.

Herbert Prochnov

❦

Family life is a bit like a runny
peach pie – not perfect
but who's complaining?

Robert Brault

A happy family is but
an earlier heaven.

George Bernard Shaw

A unit composed... of children...
men, women, an occasional
animal, and the common cold.

Ogden Nash on the definition of a family

Before I got married I had
six theories about bringing
up children; now I have six
children, and no theories.

John Wilmot

HEY BABY!

There are two things
in life for which we are
never prepared: twins.

Josh Billings

Breast feeding should not
be attempted by fathers
with hairy chests... they can
make the baby sneeze.

Mike Harding, *The Armchair Anarchist's Almanac*

Typical of Margaret. She
produced twins and avoided the
necessity of a second pregnancy.

Denis Thatcher

I spoke to Luca on the phone and he burped, I was in tears. He looks like a turnip, but a beautiful turnip.

Colin Firth

The toddler craves independence,
but he fears desertion.

Dorothy Corkville Briggs, *Your Child's Self-Esteem*

Babies are the enemies
of the human race.

Isaac Asimov

Here we have a baby. It is composed
of a bald head and a pair of lungs.

Eugene Field

Having children gives your life a purpose. Right now, my purpose is to get some sleep.

Reno Goodale

A loud noise at one end and no sense of responsibility at the other.

Ronald Knox's definition of a baby

Having a baby changes the way
you view your in-laws. I love it when
they come to visit now. They can
hold the baby and I can go out.

Matthew Broderick

———

'Diaper' backwards spells
'repaid'. Think about it.

Marshall McLuhan

TEENAGE KICKS

Teenagers are
God's punishment
for having sex.

Patrick Murray

Few things are more satisfying
than seeing your children have
teenagers of their own.

Doug Larson

Let your child be the teenager he or
she wants to be, not the adolescent
you were or wish you had been.

Laurence Steinberg and Ann Levine,
You and Your Adolescent

Adolescence begins when children stop asking questions – because they know all the answers.

Evan Esar

❧

If one of my girls walked in and said, 'Daddy, I'm going out with a footballer,' I'd say, 'No, you *were* going out with a footballer!'

Andy Gray

It's amazing. One
day you look at your
phone bill and realise
they're teenagers.

Milton Berle

The main problem with teenagers
is that they're just like their
parents were at their age.

Anonymous

An adolescent is somebody
who is in between things.
A teenager is somebody who's
kind of permanently there.

Andrew Greeley

When you are seventeen
you aren't really serious.

Arthur Rimbaud

The young always have the
same problem – how to rebel
and conform at the same time.

Quentin Crisp

The worst eternal triangle known is
teenager, parent and telephone.

Lavonne Mathison

Telling a teenager the facts of life is like giving a fish a bath.

Arnold H. Glasow

Imagination is something that sits up with Dad and Mom the first time their teenager stays out late.

Lane Olinghouse

LIKE FATHER, LIKE SON

My father had a
profound influence on
me, he was a lunatic.

Spike Milligan

William Pitt the Younger is not
only a chip off the old block
but the old block itself.

Edmund Burke

All my sons are named George
Foreman. They all know
where they came from.

George Foreman

For rarely are sons similar to their
fathers: most are worse, and a few
are better than their fathers.

Homer

A man's children and his garden
both reflect the amount of weeding
done during the growing season.

Anonymous

When a father gives to his
son, both laugh; when a son
gives to his father, both cry.

Jewish proverb

Mother would come out and say,
'You're tearing up the grass';
'We're not raising grass,' Dad
would reply. 'We're raising boys.'

Harmon Killebrew on playing rough with his dad

It is not flesh and blood but the heart
which makes us fathers and sons.

Friedrich Schiller

When you can't do anything else to a
boy, you can make him wash his face.

Ed Hove

Fathers and sons show much more
consideration towards one another
than mothers and daughters do.

Friedrich Nietzsche

I don't mind looking into the mirror and seeing my father.

Michael Douglas

I am an expert of electricity. My father occupied the chair of applied electricity at the state prison.

W. C. Fields

Dad always called me
his 'favourite son'.

Cameron Diaz on being a tomboy

MY WISE OLD MAN

It is a wise father that knows his own child.

William Shakespeare

My father gave me these hints
on speech-making: 'Be sincere...
be brief... be seated.'

James Roosevelt

My son complains about headaches.
I tell him all the time, when you
get out of bed, it's feet first!

Henny Youngman

My father considered a walk
among the mountains as the
equivalent of churchgoing.

Aldous Huxley

Parents can only give good advice
or put them on the right paths.

Anne Frank

Jarrell was not so much a father...
as an affectionate encyclopaedia.

Mary Jarrell

By the time a man realises that
maybe his father was right, he usually
has a son who thinks he's wrong.

Charles Wadsworth

Dad always thought that laughter
was the best medicine, which... is why
several of us died of tuberculosis.

Jack Handey

I didn't know the full facts of
life until I was 17. My father
never talked about his work.

Martin Freud on his father Sigmund

One father is more than
100 schoolmasters.

George Herbert

I have always had the feeling I
could do anything and my dad told
me I could. I was in college before
I found out he might be wrong.

Ann Richards

———•———

I have never been a material girl. My
father always told me never to love
anything that cannot love you back.

Imelda Marcos

———•———

As daddy said, life is 95
per cent anticipation.

Gloria Swanson

My dad has always taught me
these words: care and share.

Tiger Woods

My dad always had this little sign
on his desk: 'The bigger your head
is, the easier your shoes are to fill.'

Phil Jackson

NO. 1 DAD

When I was a kid,
I used to imagine
animals running under
my bed. I told my
dad... He cut the
legs off the bed.

Lou Brock

Being a great father is like
shaving. No matter how good
you shaved today, you have
to do it again tomorrow.

Reed Markham

What do I owe my father?
Everything.

Henry Van Dyke

I looked up to my dad. He
was always on a ladder.

David Chartrand

Dads grab themselves
a spoon and dig
right in with you.

Anonymous

Your dad is the man who does
all the heavy shovelling for your
sandcastle, and then tells you
you've done a wonderful job.

Rose O'Kelly

❦

He sewed button eyes on my teddy
bear when its other eyes fell off.

Cynthia Heimel

❦

He opened the jar of pickles
when no one else could.

Erma Bombeck

I talk to him secretly not really
knowing whether he hears, but
it makes me feel better.

Natasha Josefowitz on talking to her deceased father

None of you can ever be
proud enough of being the
child of such a father who has
not his equal in this world – so
great, so good, so faultless.

Queen Victoria

I think my dad is a lot cooler than other dads. He acts like he's still seveteen.

Miley Cyrus

He sat there and ate in the pouring rain, dripping wet, just for the hell of it.

Dick Van Dyke on his dad at a family picnic

TOUGH LOVE

My father only hit
me once – but he
used a Volvo.

Bob Monkhouse

Raising kids is part joy and
part guerrilla warfare.

Ed Asner

One motivation is worth ten threats,
two pressures and six reminders.

Paul Sweeney

Never raise your hand to your kids.
It leaves your groin unprotected.

Red Buttons

I never got along with my dad.
Kids used to come up to me and
say, 'My dad can beat up your
dad.' I'd say, 'Yeah? When?'

Bill Hicks

... my father bought me a
blunt instrument. He told
me to knock myself out.

**Jay London on the time he told his
dad he wanted to take up music**

I find that waving
the gun around
pretty much gets
the same job done.

Denis Leary on his refusal to smack his children

The sooner you treat your son as a man, the sooner he will be one.

John Dryden

Love well, whip well.

Benjamin Franklin

Children are gleeful barbarians.

Joseph Morgenstern

And my parents
finally realise that
I'm kidnapped and
they snap into action
immediately: they
rent out my room.

Woody Allen

FATHER'S PRIDE

She's more
beautiful than the
Brooklyn Bridge!

Charles Hayes on first seeing his child Mary

By profession, I am a soldier
and take pride in that fact.
But I am prouder, infinitely
prouder, to be a father.

General Douglas MacArthur

I'm not going to have a better day, a
more magical moment, than the first
time I heard my daughter giggle.

Sean Penn

Love and fear. Everything the
father of a family says must
inspire one or the other.

Joseph Joubert

Nothing I've ever done has given me more joys and rewards than being a father to my children.

Bill Cosby

Getting a burp out of your little thing is probably the greatest satisfaction I've come across.

Brad Pitt on his first child

When you have brought up kids,
there are memories you store
directly in your tear ducts.

Robert Brault

My father gave me the greatest
gift anyone could give another
person: he believed in me.

Jim Valvano

While we try to teach our children
all about life, our children teach
us what life is all about.

Angela Schwindt

———

Children are the only form of
immortality that we can be sure of.

Peter Ustinov

———

Once I had my first hit, Dad
started to introduce himself
as Nancy Sinatra's father!

Nancy Sinatra

DAD'S IN CHARGE

Well I'm his daddy...
so he answers
to me first.

Kevin Millar

A father's words are like
a thermostat that sets the
temperature in the house.

Paul Lewis

———•———

Always obey your parents,
when they are present.

Mark Twain

———•———

The voice of parents is the voice
of gods, for to their children
they are heaven's lieutenants.

William Shakespeare

Parents who are afraid to put their foot down usually have children who step on their toes.

Chinese proverb

Parents are the bones on which children sharpen their teeth.

Peter Ustinov

We all knew dad was
the one in charge:
he had control
of the remote.

Anonymous

My father was afraid of his father, I was afraid of my father, and I don't see why my children shouldn't be afraid of me.

Lord Mountbatten

You hate to say things that will upset your kids, but then sometimes you have to because you can't let them run around wild.

Ozzy Osbourne

If your children look
up to you, you've
made a success of
life's biggest job.

Anonymous

SPORTS MAD DAD

The place of
the father in the
modern suburban
family is a very small
one, particularly
if he plays golf.

Bertrand Russell

A father's solemn duty is to watch
football with his children and teach
them when to shout at the ref.

Paul Collins

'What he can't learn on the back
of a horse is not worth teaching.'

Dick Francis quoting his father

It is admirable for a
man to take his son
fishing, but there
is a special place
in heaven for the
father who takes his
daughter shopping.

John Sinor

It's not the fishin'... It's
the time together.

Anonymous

If you put a baseball and other toys
in front of a baby, he'll pick up a
baseball in preference to the others.

Tris Speaker

Dad, what do people do on
Sunday who don't play golf?

Bobby Jones to his father as a child

There are three things in my life
which I really love: God, my family,
and baseball. The only problem
– once baseball season starts, I
change the order around a bit.

Al Gallagher

DADDY OR CHIPS?

This would be a better world for children if the parents had to eat the spinach.

Groucho Marx

A compromise is the art of dividing
a cake in such a way that everyone
believes he has the biggest piece.

Ludwig Erhard

The other night I ate at a really
nice family restaurant. Every
table had an argument going.

George Carlin

Govern a family as you would
cook a small fish – very gently.

Chinese proverb

Kids are great.
They never know
when I steal a few
of their sweeties.

Anonymous

There are times when parenthood
seems nothing but feeding
the mouth that bites you.

Peter De Vries

My father was a fastidious man.
He ate a banana with
a knife and fork.

Quentin Crisp

My dad was a mean man,
he hypnotised my mother
not to order a starter.

Harry Hill

As a child my family's
menu consisted of
two choices: take
it or leave it.

Buddy Hackett

ALL YOU NEED IS LOVE

I love my dad, although
I'm definitely critical
of him sometimes,
like when his pants
are too tight.

Liv Tyler

Let your children go if you
want to keep them.

Malcolm Stevenson Forbes

I cannot understand how in the past
I managed to cope without getting
cuddled this many times a day.

Russell Crowe

Stop trying to perfect your
child, but keep trying to perfect
your relationship with him.

Dr Henker

There's no pillow
quite so soft as
a father's strong
shoulder.

Richard L. Evans

We never know the love of a parent
till we become parents ourselves.

Henry Ward Beecher

I am not ashamed to say that
no man I ever met was my
father's equal, and I never
loved any other man as much.

Hedy Lamarr

Fatherly love is the ability
to expect the best from your
children despite the facts.

Jasmine Birtles, *A Father's Little Instruction Book*

Men love their children, not
because they are promising plants,
but because they are theirs.

Charles Montagu

Children need love, especially
when they don't deserve it.

Harold Hulbert

I loved my father. I looked
for his faithful response in
the eyes of many men.

Patricia Neal

DAD'S TAXI SERVICE

A pedestrian... is a man who has two cars – one being driven by his wife and the other by one of his children.

Robert Bradbury

My dad used to spend ages tinkering under the bonnet of his Capri. Then it would invariably have to be towed to the garage to repair the damaged he'd caused.

Robert Greenway

The father is concerned with parking space, the children with outer space and the mother with closet space.

Evan Esar

Can you abandon a child along
a public highway for kicking
daddy's seat for 600 miles?

Erma Bombeck, *Chicken Soup
for the Expectant Mother*

Why don't they use a cushion?

Steven Wright on seeing a car with
a 'Baby on Board' sign

A father and his car keys
are soon parted.

Anonymous

It is amazing how quickly the
kids learn to drive a car, yet
are unable to understand the
lawnmower... or vacuum cleaner.

Ben Bergor

Children in the back seat of cars
cause accidents. And accidents in
the back seats of cars cause children.

Sid Caesar

DAD, YOU'RE SO EMBARRASSING!

Sing out loud in the
car even, or especially,
if it embarrasses
your children.

Marilyn Penland

Because of their size, parents may
be difficult to discipline properly.

P. J. O'Rourke

If my dad didn't think they
were funny, he wouldn't
let them in the house.

Mike Myers on the way his dad treated his friends

My father hated radio and he could
not wait for television to be invented
so that he could hate that too.

Peter De Vries

I was always embarrassed because
my dad wore a suit... while my friends'
parents were punks or hippies.

Shirley Manson

I'm probably going to be one
of those very embarrassing
parents who's a naturist.

Robbie Williams

To an adolescent,
there is nothing
in the world more
embarrassing
than a parent.

Dave Barry

Have you enjoyed this book?
If so, why not write a review
on your favourite website?

Thanks very much for buying
this Summersdale book.

www.summersdale.com